IF GRANDMA HAD WHEELS

IF GRANDMA

JEWISH FOLK

HAD WHEELS

SAYINGS

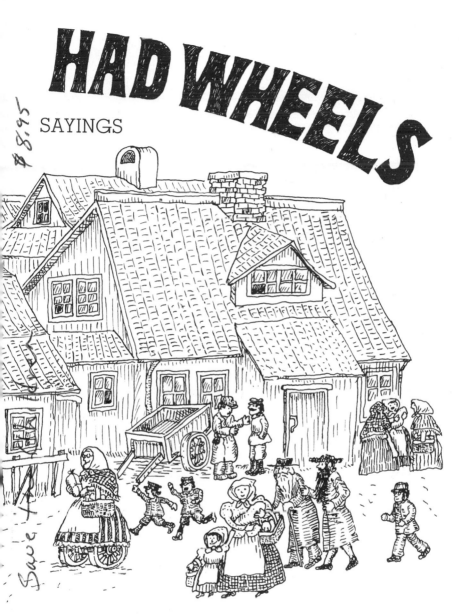

selected by Ruby G. Strauss
illustrated by Richard Rosenblum

ATHENEUM   1985   NEW YORK

ISBN 0-689-31156-7

Text copyright © 1985 by Ruby G. Strauss
Pictures copyright © 1985 by Richard Rosenblum
All rights reserved
Published simultaneously in Canada by
Collier Macmillan Canada Inc.
Printed and bound by Maple-Vail, Binghamton, N.Y.
Designed by Richard Rosenblum
First Edition

IF YOU EAT YOUR BAGEL,
YOU'LL HAVE NOTHING
LEFT BUT THE HOLE

A GOAT HAS A BEARD, BUT
THAT DOSN'T MAKE HIM
A RABBI.

IF YOU HAVE BUTTER ON
YOUR HEAD, DON'T WALK
IN THE SUN

IF YOU DON'T RUN SO FAR,

YOU CAN'T CHEW WITH
SOMEONE ELSE'S TEETH

THE WAY BACK WILL BE SHORTER.

AT NIGHT ALL COWS LOOK THE SAME

IF YOU WANT TO BE A BARBER, PRACTICE ON SOME ONE ELSE'S BEARD!

BUTTERED BREAD ALWAYS FALLS ON ITS FACE

DON'T GO INTO THE FOREST

A PERSON CAN SEE A SPECK IN ANOTHER'S HAIR, BUT CAN'T SEE A FLY ON HIS OWN NOSE

IF YOU'RE AFRAID OF LEAVES

ONE ENEMY IS ONE TOO MANY

IF CATS WORE GLOVES, THEY WOULD CATCH NO MICE

IF YOU CARRY A LIGHT, YOU'LL NOT FEAR THE DARK

IF YOU LIE DOWN WITH DOGS YOU'LL GET UP WITH FLEAS

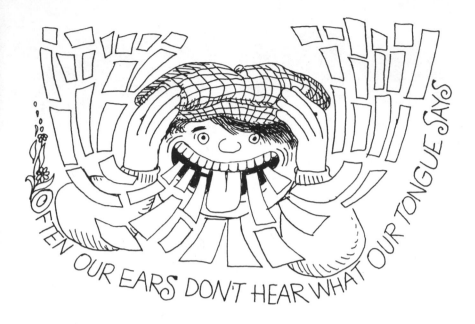

OFTEN OUR EARS DON'T HEAR WHAT OUR TONGUE SAYS

MORE PEOPLE DIE FROM OVEREATING THAN FROM HUNGER

CHARGE NOTHING AND YOU'LL GET A LOT
OF CUSTOMERS

A PERSON WHO HAS BEEN BITTEN BY A
SNAKE IS AFRAID OF A PIECE OF ROPE

IT IS EASIER TO HEAR A SECRET THAN
KEEP IT.

THE PERSON WHO GIVES LITTLE WITH
A SMILE GIVES MORE THAN THE ONE
WHO GIVES MUCH WITH A FROWN

IF I AM LIKE SOMEONE ELSE, WHO WILL BE LIKE ME?

GUESTS, LIKE FISH, BEGIN TO SMELL ON THE THIRD DAY.

IF YOU LOOK FOR CAKE, YOU'LL LOSE
YOUR BREAD

DON'T COUNT THE TEETH

YOU NEED LUCK TO INHERIT BRAINS

IN SOMEONE ELSE'S MOUTH

WHEN YOU QUARREL, DO
IT IN SUCH A WAY THAT
YOU CAN MAKE UP

TOO MANY CAPTAINS WILL SINK A
SHIP

AN ERROR, ONCE LEARNED, IS HARD
TO UNLEARN

YOU CAN'T FILL A SACK THAT
IS FULL OF HOLES

Asking charity from a miser is like fishing in the desert

When brains are needed, muscles won't do

LOVE THY NEIGHBOR, EVEN
WHEN HE PLAYS THE TROMBONE

A LIAR TELLS HIS STORY
SO OFTEN THAT HE BEGINS
TO BELIEVE IT HIMSELF

WHEN TWO PLAY, ONE MUST
WIN AND ONE MUST LOSE

A TREE CAN'T BE FELLED WITH ONE STROKE

LOCKS KEEP OUT ONLY THE HONEST

WHAT THREE KNOW IS NO LONGER A SECRET

BETTER A LITTLE PUMPKIN IN
YOUR HAND THAN A BIG ONE
IN THE FIELD

WHEN TWO QUARREL, THE THIRD GRABS THE
HAT

THE ONLY THING FREE IS GARBAGE

IF YOU HAVE NOTHING TO SAY, SAY NOTHING

WHEN A PERSON DOSN'T KNOW HOW TO
DANCE, SHE SAYS THE MUSICIANS
DON'T KNOW HOW TO PLAY

IF ONE PERSON SAYS YOU'RE A DONKEY, DON'T MIND. IF TWO SAY SO, BE WORRIED. IF THREE SAY SO, GO BUY YOURSELF A SADDLE.

IT IS BETTER TO ASK THE WAY FIFTY TIMES

CUCKOO

TICK TICK TICK TICK

TICK TICK

BONG BONG BONG BONG

EVEN A STOPPED CLOCK IS RIGHT TWICE A DAY

THAN TO TAKE THE WRONG ROAD ONCE

IF GRANDMA HAD WHEELS
SHE'D BE A WAGON